Terrific Trucks!

FOOD TRUCKS

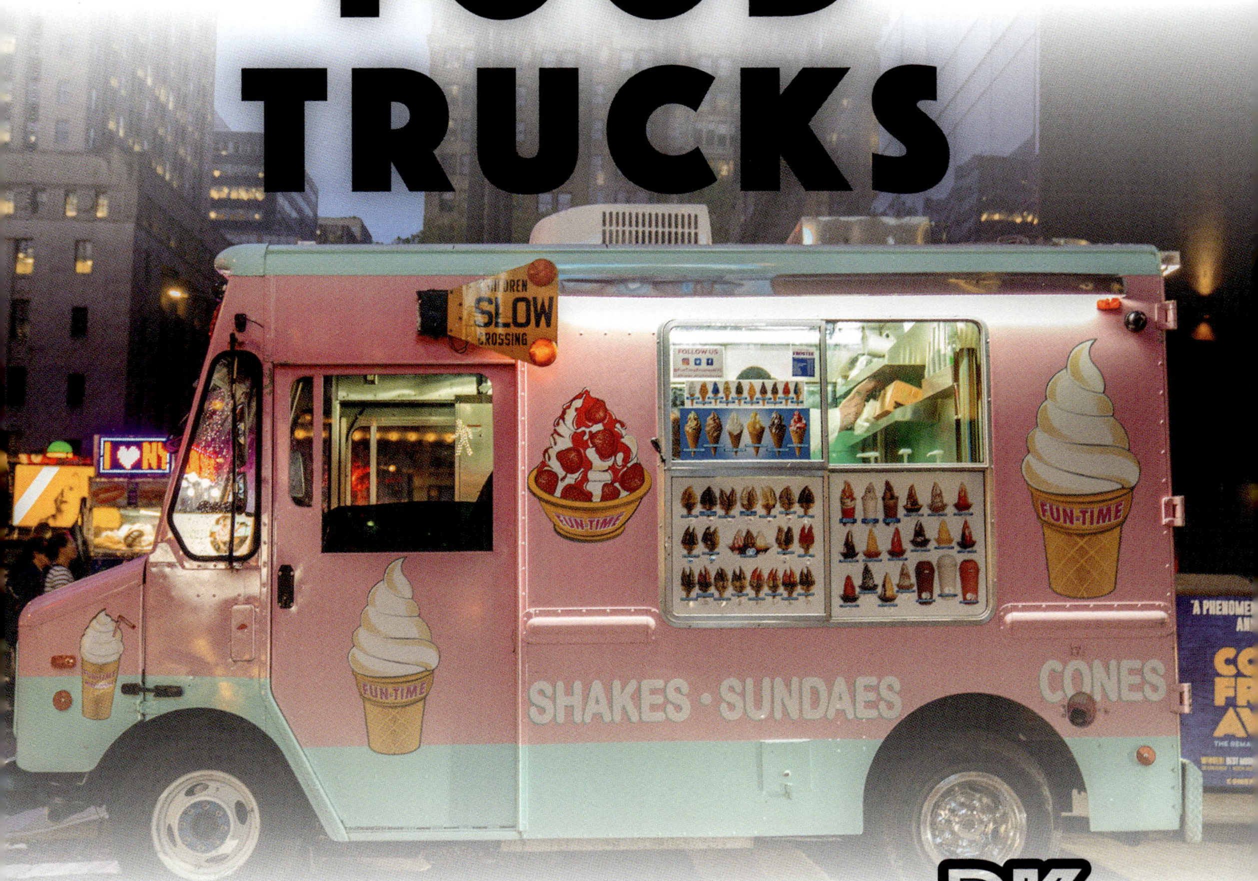

Ursula Pang

PowerKiDS press

PK Beginners

Look at the food trucks!

PHILLY'S
CHEESE STEAK
ELITE
FRESHPITA
HALAL

Food trucks sell food.

SAUSAGES
SERVING TORONTO
FOR OVER 30 YEARS!
BURGERS
FRIES
French Fries
Supreme Fries
Poutine
Sausage
Hot Dog
Burger
Beverage
PASS
HOT DOG
& FRIES
$5.00
Hot Dog
$2.99
Sausage
$3.99
FREE
POP
$1.00
SMALL 4.50
5.50
6.50

Food trucks are moving kitchens.

Food truck kitchens are small!

This food truck makes eggs.

This food truck sells tacos.

TACOS OPEN
TACOS
(929) 34
CALL TO ORDER
Especiales Birria
Beverages

This food truck sells pizza.

This food truck sells ice cream!

FUN-TIME
CONES
SHAKES · SUNDAES
FUN-TIME
SMOOTHIE INC.
328 TEN-EYCK ST.

Mom pays
for our food.

Workers clean the food truck.

Street eat

The food truck drives away!

ICE CREAM

Published in 2026 by The Rosen Publishing Group, Inc.
2544 Clinton Street, Buffalo, NY 14224

First Edition

Editor: Greg Roza
Book Design: Jeffrey Taylor

Photo Credits: Cover Pandora Pictures/Shutterstock.com; p. 3 Andriy Blokhin/Shutterstock.com; p. 5 hecke61/Shutterstock.com; p. 7 AI Generated image/Shutterstock.com; p. 9 antoniodiaz/Shutterstock.com; p. 11 MPH Photos/Shutterstock.com; p. 13 Plat-Q/Shutterstock.com; p. 15 CREATISTA/Shutterstock.com; p. 17 Janet Julie Vanatko/Shutterstock.com; p. 19 Artem Varnitsin/Shutterstock.com; p. 21 Pressmaster/Shutterstock.com; p. 23 AI Generated image/Shutterstock.com.

Library of Congress Cataloging-in-Publication Data

Names: Pang, Ursula, author.
Title: Food trucks / Ursula Pang.
Description: Buffalo : PowerKids Press, 2025. | Series: Terrific trucks!
Identifiers: LCCN 2024053769 (print) | LCCN 2024053770 (ebook) | ISBN 9781499451689 (library binding) | ISBN 9781499451672 (paperback) | ISBN 9781499451696 (ebook)
Subjects: LCSH: Food trucks--Juvenile literature.
Classification: LCC TX945.35 .P36 2025 (print) | LCC TX945.35 (ebook) | DDC 641.5--dc23/eng/20250131
LC record available at https://lccn.loc.gov/2024053769
LC ebook record available at https://lccn.loc.gov/2024053770

Manufactured in the United States of America